Healthy
Leaders

Keith E. Yoder

House to House Publications
1924 West Main Street • Ephrata, Pennsylvania 17522

Copyright © 1998 by House to House Publications
Second Printing: 2001
1924 West Main Street
Ephrata, Pennsylvania 17522
Tele: 717-738-3751 or 800-848-5892

ISBN 1-886973-31-8

Dedicated with affection to
those who serve
in the responsibility of leadership
to influence others toward Godly purposes

and to Marian, my wife,
whose leadership challenges and encourages
others to excellence.

Acknowledgments

We are indebted to numerous individuals for the knowledge we have. To communicate our knowledge through a text such as this, is similarly a joint effort.

It is my joy to acknowledge the encouragement of more than a score of individuals who believed the Lord wanted this book to be written. Steve Prokopchak and others at House to House Publications gave their encouragement and expertise to bring the work to its final form—namely, Larry Kreider, Sarah Mohler and Karen Ruiz.

Many thanks to Bob Petersheim, Cindy Riker, Don Riker and Marian Yoder, my close associates who helped to clarify the way the convictions presented here are communicated.

I am grateful for what I have learned from working with men and women in responsibilities of leadership; some of their experiences are illustrated on these pages.

Harold Eberle opened my understanding to creative perspectives in responsibilities of leadership in his visionary work, *God's Leaders For Tomorrow's World.*

Several significant concepts regarding leadership were introduced to me by the late Edwin Friedman who, in his remarks, pointed me to Jesus Christ who embodies these truths to the fullest.

Apart from Jesus Christ, our view of the world, and leadership, is eccentric (off-center). In Him are hidden all the treasures of wisdom and knowledge. Join me in considering the Word in the words that follow.

Contents

Foreword

Several years ago I was ready to quit. I had served as the Senior Pastor of a church that had grown from a handful of believers to over 2000, but I had come to an impasse. Most of my struggle involved my apparent inability to work in harmony with some members of our leadership team.

In the midst of this turmoil, I met with my friend Keith Yoder. I had known Keith for years and admired his ability to "cut to the chase" to help pastors and leaders deal with the real issues confronting them. This time I was not just observing; I was desperate.

Keith helped me to understand how the Lord had "wired" me. He showed me how to be secure in my relationship with Christ and His call on my life as a servant leader. I learned practical biblical keys to understand other leaders with differing gifts and abilities.

Since Keith fathered me through a process of healing and served as a mentor, I have found myself compelled by the Father to do the same—to be a spiritual father and mentor to others. Much of what I have learned from Keith during this vital season of growth in my life can be found within the pages of this book.

I recommend *Healthy Leaders* to Christian leaders and future leaders everywhere. Don't wait until you face a crisis. Allow the Lord to use the truths in this book to lay a foundation in your life for your present and future role of leadership in the body of Christ. Become the healthy leader the Lord has ordained you to be.

Larry Kreider
DOVE Christian Fellowship International Director

Introduction

L eadership is vital. The quality of life and the productivity of every group rises and falls in relationship to the effectiveness of its leadership. This is true in families, businesses, churches, synagogues, community organizations and civil governments.

Learning to lead may seem overwhelming. There are several options to help leaders to become more effective. We can study a wide range of *theories* of leadership. Or we can consider a multitude of *principles* mined from experience by successful leaders throughout the centuries. We may seek to emulate *models*, contemporary leaders, who are successful in our field of endeavor.

Effective leadership is not borrowed. While there is much to learn from how others lead, the foundational conviction of this text maintains that effective leaders are persons who have a clear sense of identity and direction. They are persons with a healthy sense of individuality by which they can influence others in a wholesome way. Hence, the title, *Healthy Leaders.*

Identity and intimacy are linked. Leaders are empowered most fully as their identity is established in a personal relationship with and a revelation from God. That relationship is demonstrated to us and made possible for us through the relationship of Jesus Christ and the Father.

Your identity becomes your influence. Are you in a crisis regarding your leadership? There is hope. Do you need to revitalize your influence upon others? There is a way. Are you an emerging leader seeking to avoid pitfalls and fulfill your destiny? There is wisdom. Do you desire to mentor a new generation of leaders?

There is a path to follow.

Sensitivity to leaders is important. At some places in the text, I have changed the names of people where protecting their identity seemed advisable. Also, to facilitate the reading of this book, I generally used the masculine gender when referring to leaders. For the record, I believe that both women and men are given spiritual mandates to lead.

And now, let me introduce you to Glen . . .

Keith E. Yoder
Teaching the Word Ministries
Leola, PA

Chapter 1

A Clear
Sense of Identity

Glen had been pastor at Grace Church for approximately a year when the "honeymoon period" ended. Some of the "old guard" members on the board began to resist his new initiatives. False accusations began surfacing from the rumor mill.

Glen was not surprised, nor was he swayed by the turn of events. He knew God had called him to Grace Church. Without defending himself, he kept clarifying his vision in his preaching and in one-to-one lunches with key leaders. He stood firm in his convictions, remained friendly to all, and prayed.

As the weeks unfolded more of the story, it became apparent that his resistance from the board was traceable to one uninvolved businessman who did not like the new preacher's style of leadership.

When the time for election of church board members arrived, there was no clear indication as to what the result would be. Glen prayed and waited without compromising the direction he was convinced the Lord had given him for this congregation.

Without campaigning, without manipulation on Glen's part, miraculously the mood of the congregation changed. In the election the "old guard" were replaced, and one younger leader repented of his rebellious attitude. The new board became more responsive to Glen's leadership.

While many church conflicts are not resolved in this manner, this one was, in part, because the leader had a clear sense of who he was. His identity did not shift in the midst of resistance to his sense of purpose.

Leaders who are effective have a healthy sense of individuality. An effective leader is one who has a clear sense of identity as a person because he has an intimate relationship with his heavenly Father. The Lord Jesus embodied healthy individuality throughout His entire ministry. If we want to lead the way the Lord wants us to, we need to embrace this important principle of leadership. Knowing who we are will bring a fresh release and responsibility to our ministries, causing people to appreciate us much more as leaders and allowing us to move forward in the area of responsibility God has given us.

> **Leaders who are effective have a healthy sense of individuality. An effective leader is one who has a clear sense of identity as a person because he has an intimate relationship with his heavenly Father**

As we look at Jesus as a leader, we can learn some very significant things. First of all, in His anointing and in His lordship, Jesus is not only the Christ, He is also a man—a person.

In John 13:1, we read that Jesus knew that the hour of giving Himself as a sacrifice for the world had come. It was the primary purpose for which He came, and now He was leaving His disciples and a phase of His ministry was ending. He was going to face the most difficult task that any human being has ever faced. He knew He had come from God and could deal with what was coming up, even though a little while later He would be agonizing in the Garden in a very human way, pleading, "Do I have to go through this? Is there some other way?"

Jesus was the vessel—the earthen humanity through which God Himself worked to demonstrate that we, also, can walk as He walked. And as leaders, we also can lead as He led.

Love, our motivation

Love needs to be our primary motivation in leadership. We need to love unconditionally, as Jesus did. Jesus loved His disciples through it all, *"having loved His own who were in the world, He loved them to the end"* (John 13:1). He didn't just love them through a certain period of time of His ministry, but he loved them to the fullest extent right up until the time He would depart from this world. When this concept is translated to Swahili, I am told it describes a picture of the horizon. Jesus loved His disciples "unto the horizon." When one looks to the horizon, that apparent junction of earth and sky, it extends on and on. And so we get the idea that Jesus loved to the fullest extent—without end.

In this context of loving them, He demonstrated His healthy sense of individuality by revealing three important things about Himself: He showed He knew His purpose, He knew His identity, and He knew His roots.

> *"And during supper, the devil having already put into the heart of Judas Iscariot, the son of Simon, to betray Him, Jesus, **knowing that the Father had given all things into His hands, and that He had come forth from God, and was going back to God,** rose from supper, and laid aside His garments; and taking a towel, He girded Himself about. Then He poured water into the basin, and began to wash the disciples' feet"* (John 13:2-5, emphasis mine).

Jesus knew His purpose

Jesus clearly knew His purpose. Verse three says Jesus knew the Father had "given all things into His hands." The Father had entrusted Him with responsibilities. Everything that He needed was there at His disposal from the Father. He understood what His role was. He knew what His relationship with His Father was in reference to what He had been given. He didn't grasp His role. It was given to Him by the Father—a stewardship for which He needed to care.

Jesus knew His identity and His roots

In verse three, we see that Jesus knew, *"He had come forth from God."* He knew His source, reservoir and identity was rooted in God Himself. He was God, but He knew He, as a person, Jesus, had come from God. He was sent from somewhere. He was not merely doing something that He wanted to do; He had a commission. He was an ambassador (sent out). He was not a floating, itinerant minister with no roots and no relationships— He was "covered back home." He had come from God.

Jesus knew where He was going

Jesus knew He was "going back to God" according to verse three. He knew where He had come from—His identity, His roots. Now He was going home. People in the world need to know their roots and where they are going. Human beings still need to know the answer to life's questions: "Who am I? Where did I come from? Where am I going?" Jesus knew the answers to those questions, and those answers came out of an intimate relationship with His heavenly Father. He knew who He was because of that intimate, close, personal relationship with His Father that was sustained by daily prayer and listening to His Father's will.

Since we cannot cut ourselves off entirely from our past, we cannot ignore our roots, or take them lightly. We need to look honestly at every part of our experience—even those painful ones—and face who we are. We should never deny where we came from or despise our roots. To do so would be foolish. We need to acknowledge where we came from, accept it for what it is, and build and grow from it.

Of course, a plant is not just roots. It develops all the way to fruit. Jesus knew His past and where He was going—He was going back to God. We, too, need this same appreciation and understanding of our past, because it gives us hope for the future.

While on earth, Jesus identified with what it is like to be one of us. And now, we can identify with what it is like to lead as He led, by His example.

Ask the hard questions

If we, as leaders, are grappling with understanding our past or where we are going, it is critical to seek the Lord's guidance and the help of brothers and sisters in answering those questions. When those answers are not clear to us, we cannot lead with clarity and decisiveness. Instead, we impose our problems on those whom we are responsible to lead.

Ervan had been the pastor for several years when the issues in his life began to surface, not only in the home, but also in the congregation. Attendance was declining, administration was unclear, and people were frustrated with several unsuccessful "new directions" over the last five years.

Ervan seemed to ride the fence on issues, not wanting to offend people who may disagree or who may reject him. His fear of rejection emerged whenever a controversial issue arose.

While the people loved their pastor as a person, some of them became increasingly frustrated with his leadership. The confusion, the vacillation, and the unresolved fears within him spilled over into the persona of the congregation.

During times of change and transition, things can get rather foggy and confusing. Especially during those times, we need to depend fully on God's grace to again define who we are, where we came from, and where we are going. It is important that we keep considering those questions because they are foundational to our ability to lead God's people.

Tom and his wife sat across the living room from me as we began to sort through the changes and resulting transition in his life. He was struggling with who he was after several years as a successful university football coach. As a coach, he had been energized by all the things to be done every week and month of the year to keep a successful program growing. Now that he had laid down the coaching position, he was experiencing an alarming sense of emptiness, worthlessness, and confusion.

In short, his identity had become so associated with his role as coach that he had "lost himself" in the process. Now the Lord led him into a season where his identity would be more shaped by "being" than by "doing." He was faced with the question, "Who am I?"

Healthy individuality

As we have learned, Jesus had a clear definition of Himself. He also had clear direction of where He was going and what He was doing. This is foundational to the principle of healthy individuality. A healthy individual has a sense of who he is and where he is going. Therefore, that person can lead and influence others effectively. It causes a chain reaction within the group being led to also know who they are and where they are going.

It all comes back to leadership. Leadership is a precious gift. It is the influence that moves a group from where it is to where it must go. The countries that have good leadership can handle their problems effectively. Countries that have weak leadership (self-oriented and politically-based in motivation), struggle in terms of their moral fiber and capacity to solve their problems.

Leadership is dealing with problems

When we sign up for leadership, we sign up to deal with problems. Leadership is not merely an honorary position. Much of leadership is being involved in the lives of people, complete with problems.

Willette is a leader who nurtured the local Crisis Pregnancy Center into a respected ministry. She overcame zoning hassles, political intrigue, community misunderstandings, and financial crises because she remained true to her conviction that God had chosen her for this work. She kept her focus intact—on the needs of young women and their families who needed support. Now the phone calls that beckon her are from the directors of other Crisis Pregnancy Centers who seek her counsel on problem areas in their ministries. She has become a leader among leaders.

To solve problems, one must have a measure of decisiveness. Our ability to be decisive is linked to the clarity of our identity.

Leadership is a precious gift

Whatever the realm of society and the number of people we lead, we cannot escape realizing how precious leadership is in the midst of those people. Whether it be in a family, an extended family, a congregation, a community, or a nation—the gift of leadership is very precious to that group. As leaders, we must realize the investment people and God are making in us as leaders. We are a special gift, and how we function determines the extent to which our leadership is released to bless that group.

Leadership is a spiritual reality

The leadership that we exercise is a mystery, a spiritual substance. It is one thing to be called a leader and to be in the position of leader, it is another thing to actually exude and exercise leadership. Leadership is that precious, fragrant ointment that graces a group and enables ministry to happen in a constructive way.

In one instance, I consulted with a congregation and their leadership team. The leadership was endeavoring to work as a team, but the situation was frustrating. Each leader, in his own right, was excellent in character and a good leader, but somehow the mix of the group did not produce leadership. We had leaders, but we did not have the flow of unified leadership.

Leadership is a precious, spiritual reality that comes from those who know who they are and the direction they are going. When there is confusion about those two things, then the grace, fragrance, anointing and impact of leadership wanes. Leadership is a stewardship of something God has given to us in our hands. We need to exercise it out of a healthy sense of individuality.

Leadership has a clear purpose

When Jesus washed His disciples' feet, He knew what He was doing when He took that towel and girded Himself. He knew the direction He was going when He picked up that basin. He knew who He was when He washed those feet. He did not wash the disciples' feet because nobody else had done it yet. He had a clear purpose in mind, and it did not embarrass Him at all to do something that was not customarily His role in the situation.

We recognize that Jesus knew where He was coming from and knew where He was going. We also may be confident in our leadership because we are clear in our identity and direction. This is not to say we should be autocratic, dogmatic, bullheaded, or insensitive. Rather, we need to know who we are from an intimate relationship with God. Then we will have a sense of purpose because we have heard His voice speaking to our hearts.

A leader's role

Jesus knew who He was, so He could fulfill any role. He could wash feet or preach a sermon to 5000 people and give them a picnic lunch. He knew who He was, the direction He was going, and why He was doing what He was doing. His leadership role did not limit Him to any particular image of Himself as to what leaders do and what leaders do not do.

I once served on a commission of a denomination with representatives from throughout North America. At our first meeting located in a hotel near a large metropolitan airport, I was caught up with the importance of being appointed to the commission.

The Chair of the commission was well-educated, highly respected, and a skillful moderator. I was aware of his merits. I was about to be challenged by the measure of his Christ-likeness. While the members sat around the table waiting to make important decisions, he rose from his chair, took a pitcher of ice water in hand, and began going around the table filling a glass for each of us.

Like Jesus, our leader had a clear sense of identity and took upon himself a task of serving. His identity as a leader was not subject to the task he was doing; to the contrary, he was free to do any task, if necessary. The imprint of his humility has been branded upon my heart since that day.

We need to break down the deception that has controlled our minds into thinking that somehow, as leaders, we have a privileged few things we do and other people do the rest. We need to do whatever needs to be done, based on a clear sense of direction and identity.

When Jesus washed the disciples' feet, Peter told Jesus that He should not be doing it. Jesus reflects on Peter's statement in John 13:13-14,

> *"You call me Teacher and Lord; and you are right, for so I am. If I then, the Lord and the Teacher, washed your feet, you also ought to wash one another's feet."*

Notice Jesus did not cease to be a teacher and master while He washed their feet. He did what He did and retained His role as teacher and as master, even as He reasoned with Peter. When Peter said, "Never shall You wash my feet," Jesus said, "If I do not wash you, you have no part with Me" (verse 8). Jesus was teaching Peter something important—*If I do not do this, you are not identified with Me; that is, you not a companion in fellowship with Me.*

Healthy leaders deliberately lead, but with humility

Often we have interpreted this passage of Scripture into terms of servanthood that are divorced from the Biblical sense of the words. As a result, we promote a mild style of leadership that makes a leader a target for every person who disagrees with him. If we believe leaders are supposed to be nice people who never create waves, when someone disagrees with us, we will think, "I'll just do whatever they want me to do." That is not healthy.

Jesus did not say, "Okay, Peter, if you do not want me to wash your feet, I will not because I am just a servant." That view of being a servant has covered over much truth in this passage of Scripture. Jesus *deliberately* took the role of a servant because He knew who He was and *maintained His sense of leadership as He served.* He served by leading; He led by serving. He did not cease to be the leader when He served.

When we serve, we are still leading. When we lead, we are serving. We do not cease to lead when we serve. Jesus did not let Peter argue Him out of what He was doing. He did not let Peter's limited understanding distract Him from following through with the direction He had chosen—to wash the disciples' feet.

I witnessed a healthy example of a servant-leader at a mountain retreat. Our group was the first to arrive at the campsite that season, and some quick work was needed around the camp in order to get it ready for the rest of the folks soon to be arriving. As I walked around the corner of the building, there was our leader, Alvin, carrying a big log on his shoulder for the fire. He was the leader and was the first to serve. He knew the direction to take and knew what he was doing. He was getting this campsite ready physically in anticipation for what the Lord would do there spiritually.

Jesus deliberately took the role of a servant because He knew who He was and maintained His sense of leadership as He served. He served by leading; He led by serving.

That is the role of a true leader. To serve does not mean that you lay down your identity as the leader in the situation. To do so may result in anarchy or confusion within the group. While we as leaders do any active service, we are still leaders. Jesus *taught* Peter about what it meant to be clean, what it meant to be a part of Him and why that identity with Him is so important—even as He washed Peter's feet.

Dealing with reactions to our leadership

Notice Jesus was not moved by the reaction of Peter when Peter did not understand the direction that Jesus had taken. Sometimes, when we begin to take people in a new direction, they will react to it. Some will see the vision with us and want to go along. Other people will not be too sure about it, while others' defenses go up. Still others may react in ways that undermine the direction we are taking in hopes that things can stay the same.

The goal of a healthy leader is to not be moved by those reactions. The goal is to remain calm and at peace because we know who we are and that we are doing what God has spoken to us. As we remain calm, the impact of what God has given us to do can begin to work and establish itself until people, themselves, realize more fully the purpose of God in the situation.

Notice that Jesus was not detracted, rebuffed, or personally shaken through this interaction with Peter. He still knew that He was the Teacher and Master. Jesus dealt with Peter's reaction and it did not detract Him from knowing who He was and the direction He was taking. One of the tests of leadership is how we respond when people react to our leadership.

As leaders, do we cave in, get upset, angry, or blow up when people react to our leadership? Do we run away and hide? Or do we remain calm and peaceful because we know who we are and we know the direction we are taking?

We must not depend upon people liking us in order to know who we are and to feel good about God's calling on our lives. If we are subject to the reactions of those we lead, we will not lead well. We will not enjoy our leadership responsibility very much either.

How our relationship with our parents can affect our relationship with God

It is quite commonly understood that our relationship with our biological or adoptive parents has a lot to do with our understanding of God. It shapes our concept of fathering and mothering.

The concept we have of a person—how we understand that person, what we know about them, what we believe about them—

determines the kind of relationship we have with that person. So too, the concept we have of God shapes our relationship with Him. It is important to have a good perspective, interpretation, and understanding of our relationship with our earthly fathers. The goal ultimately is, even if we cannot positively resolve difficulties in relationships with our parents, that we have a personal, intimate relationship with the one Father of us all, God Himself. That is what Jesus had, and that was the foundation of His healthy approach to leadership.

As much as lies within us, we need to work constructively at relationships with our parents in order to relate to them in forgiveness and honor. Ephesians 6:2-3 commands, *"Honor your father and mother . . . that it may be well with you, and that you may live long on the earth."* Whether our parents did a great parenting job or not—how we relate to our parents is an expression of how we relate to the principle of authority.

Often the degree to which things go well in our lives is the degree to which we are honoring our parents. The degree to which things do not go well in a person's life may, typically, be traced back to some difficulty in honoring one's parents. Sometimes when the path has been rough and rugged between parents and children, people may experience tragedy and trouble after trouble in their lives. In such cases, it is essential to look at the principle of honoring one's parents and be scrupulous in finding every way possible to more fully honor them, living or deceased. We are to honor our parents as long as we live. Jesus honored His Father, and we also have His grace to honor our parents.

A healthy relationship with the Lord

Jesus prayed in John 17 that the same love which He shared with the Father would be in us. Think of that! The same kind of healthy love relationship that the Father and Son share, that is what

Jesus prayed we would have with the Father. We can have the same affirming, intimate, blessed, affectionate relationship with the Father as Jesus did. As leaders, we need to let our love pour out to Him. We need to embrace that intimacy in our time with Him.

Jesus knew who He was. He had a purpose, and He did not react to the reactions of others. This is the principle of healthy individuality. If we can get this truth embedded in our frame of mind, it will guide us in solving specific dilemmas. It will aid us in solving problems, and it will enable us to handle the reactions that invariably will come. It will allow us to be one step ahead, to have the alertness we need to know how to handle a situation.

The religious leaders of His day, the Pharisees and Saducees, threw many accusations at Jesus. But He was not afraid to acknowledge, "I am the Son of God." That is healthy, not prideful. When you are being buffeted with all kinds of accusations, you need to be able to say, "I know who I am. I will not be shaken by these accusations." When you are tempted with evil, you need to be able to say, "This is who I am. I do not do those things."

Remember who you are

Several years ago, I desperately prayed regularly that I would increase in a particular fruit of the Spirit. During that period of time when I failed to show that fruit of the Spirit in various situations, the Holy Spirit would whisper in my mind and my heart, "Remember who you are." There was no condemnation from Him, just a reminder, "Remember who you are." And that began helping me to overcome. Soon it got to the point when I was tempted to respond negatively, before I could act, I could hear His voice saying to me, "Remember who you are." With that grace and strength, I could avoid doing the thing I was committed to avoiding. You see, it is who we are in a relationship with the Heavenly Father that counts.

And when we know that, we do not have to react or get upset by the reactions of others.

Jesus was totally misunderstood. And even to this day, with His name being used in vain millions of times every day, He is interceding. He does not think, "Oh, these people do not understand that I am God." That would be ridiculous and unimaginable. How can the most compassionate Person in the universe, the most sensitive, delicate Person not be offended when millions of people every day are treating Him with disrespect and disregard? We now know—He knows who He is—He does not have to get upset.

We know the One who knows who He is. As we fellowship with Him, worship the Father, and dwell in the intimacy of His presence, we become like Him.

Being with Jesus determines who we are

Again notice, Jesus' identity as an individual is directly linked to His relationship with Someone else—His Father. Our identity is directly linked with being with Someone. When we are spending time with Jesus, talking to Him, declaring His words, we will know who we are. Our identity is in Jesus. Jesus came to show us the Father so our identity may be established by the Father also.

Notice the act of service Jesus did in washing the disciples' feet is reminiscent of His greater purpose as described in Philippians 2:5-8. It is just a little picture of the bigger picture. As you read this, picture in your mind Jesus taking the towel and the basin and washing the disciples' feet. Then, picture in your mind a heavenly realm where Jesus lays down His garments and picks up the tools of service.

Jesus knew who He was. He was not grasping to be God. God had given Him something to do, so He laid aside His garments just as He did in washing the disciples' feet. He took upon Himself the limitations and the role of a servant and carried out the task of sacrificially giving Himself. He knew who He was and was safe and secure that His Father would be there, on the other side of death, to raise Him up again.

Qualified as a leader

Because Jesus sacrificially gave Himself for all mankind, He was qualified to be given authority over all mankind (Philippians 2:9-11). As leaders, our sacrificial love will give life to people. A husband will give life to his wife. Parents will give life to their children. Teachers will give life to their students, cell leaders to their cells, elders to their church body, and department leaders will give life, direction and encouragement to their department. People seek life. They are drawn to where the life is.

People are looking for love; God is love. Every pre-Christian and Christian is looking for life through an intimate relationship with God their Father, although some may look in wrong places.

People will be led to life if we as leaders are in an intimate relationship with the Father Himself, particularly when we know who we are and the direction we are going without reacting when others react to us. This enduring principle of becoming a healthy individual will accomplish more in our leadership and ministry than the latest seminar on the techniques of someone else.

If we know who we are and the direction we are going, we can profit from the techniques of others. But if we do not know who we are and the direction we are going, we will bow down to the idol of another's techniques. To do so is to grasp for something that is not integral to us. The result may be more confusion because the technique does not arise from an established identity of the one who is leading.

Do not try to be someone else

Each person has a certain identity as a leader—our personality contributes to that, the kind of leadership gifts we have, the calling of God on our lives, the way we relate to authority, the way we have been parented, the way we may parent—everything goes into making up our style of influencing and leading other people. This unique blend, that comprises us, is stored deep within us, most of it unconscious.

Sometimes, however, leaders hear about someone who is an effective leader so they read his book, go to her seminar, watch how she does it, or visit his church. Although it does not hurt to observe another's leadership style, we are denying what is really in our inner being if we try to copy another's style. It is like mentally putting on Saul's armor instead of being a David (ourselves)—the way God called us.

Kurt and Bobbie started a fellowship in their home, reaching hurting people in an informal ministry style. Over the years, their "Mom and Pop" approach nurtured many folks to wholeness. As a more formal congregation emerged and grew, a team of mature leaders was developed. These dedicated team members worked alongside Kurt and Bobbie, taking full ownership of the vision.

More sophisticated organization was introduced by younger leaders. Kurt inspired the team with the ideas for growth he gleaned from seminars, videos, books and speakers. A team approach to decision-making was promoted.

But when crises arose, Kurt and Bobbie would consistently consult with each other and make decisions since it was convenient and they cared deeply. There were several instances when "Mom and Pop" violated the understanding the team had as to how decisions were to be made.

Gradually, the couples on the team became disillusioned and resigned from leadership. As they viewed it, leaders they loved deeply as persons lacked the integrity to make decisions the way they had taught the team to do. As Kurt and Bobbie returned to the real leadership style in their hearts, the congregation recovered and began to meet the needs of folk as it had in the formative years of the ministry.

We may try to "put on" somebody else's techniques, seminars and concepts, and believe in these things with our minds, but when we are in a crisis we typically respond in the natural style, within our own identity. When the pressure is on, we most often revert to our own innate style and lead "our" way. As a result, we develop an integrity problem. We have conformed to someone else's pattern outwardly, and trained the leaders around us accordingly, but then we reverted back to our own style. To do so violates the very thing we have taught the leaders we are equipping. Typically, the havoc created in these situations may disillusion and dismantle an entire generation of leaders within the organization.

As leaders who know that our identity is shaped out of our own relationship with God, we will be able to carry through and maintain this posture even in a crisis. Under pressure or under resistance, we will be the same person. The consistency and integrity of such leadership will bring security and maintain clear direction for those being led.

Summary

Let us focus on what we have established so far. Jesus had the foundation of an affectionate, affirming relationship with His heavenly Father. Therefore, He was a healthy individual. The foundation for each one of us to be a healthy person is having a personal, intimate relationship with our heavenly Father.

As the body of Christ, we can truly help one another grow up in Christ by building that intimate relationship with our Father. The happier we are as individuals, the better we can relate to other people. Paul confirms this in Philippians 2:1-5,

"If therefore there is any encouragement in Christ, if there is any consolation of love, if there is any fellowship of the Spirit, if any affection and compassion, make my joy complete by being of the same mind, maintaining the same love, united in spirit, intent on one purpose. Do nothing from selfishness or empty conceit, but with humility of mind let each of you regard one another as more important than himself; do not merely look out for your own personal interests, but also for the interests of others. Have this attitude in yourselves which was also in Christ Jesus."

The person who has difficulty putting the interest of others ahead of his own, or who has difficulty forming a common purpose with others, is someone who is wrapped up in himself and confused about his own identity. A healthy individual gives to others rather than constantly drawing from them. When we are healthy individuals, we help to form healthy marriages, families, congregations, ministries, businesses, communities, and nations.

Chapter 1
Reflections

Relationship: Intimacy

1. Have I trusted Christ as the only way to God the Father?

2. Have I found security in the truth that God loves me?

3. Have I found affirmation through hearing His voice in Scripture, in my own mind and/or through others?

Definition: Who I am

1. Who has God said that I am?

2. What values and beliefs are most important to me?

3. What abilities and spiritual gifts are evident in me?

4. What strengths and weaknesses can I acknowledge?

5. Whom has God entrusted to me to serve and influence?

Direction: Where I am going

1. What is the passion that guides my life?

2. What is the vision I have for my areas of responsibility?

3. What is the course of action I am to present to those whom the Lord would have me lead?

Chapter 2

Direction
In Leadership

Toni was a vibrant executive director. She maintained a close working relationship with the Board, honored the founders, and inspired a growing staff. At each critical point of growth in the ministry, her influence was felt in taking courageous steps into new ventures.

Personally, she faced her own challenges of unfulfilled expectations and promises, but her influence in the organization came from rich times of prayer. Her own pursuit of relationship with the Lord was fervent and transparent. She tested her ideas through a broad range of counsel with Godly advisors. When she presented her proposals to the Board, she spoke with the conviction that the Lord had given direction to her and to the ministry.

Providing leadership involves more than having meetings, solving problems and making decisions. Being a leader is more than a position. A leadership dynamic happens when there is a life-giving force, a fragrance of influence that propels a group forward in their pursuit of Godly purposes. Real leadership occurs when there is a dimension of genuine spiritual leadership imparted to us as leaders from the Lord. We need to be filled with the very life of Christ

Himself, or we will just be going through the motions and getting worn out.

As we have learned already, a healthy leader is an individual who knows who he is and the direction he is going. He or she leads with confidence and self-awareness, not reacting to how people respond to him or the direction he takes.

Clear direction in leadership

Having a clear sense of direction is one of the dimensions of healthy individuality in leadership. This is exemplified by Jesus, who knew who He was and the direction He was taking. Therefore, He was at peace when others reacted to who He said He was or the direction He said He was taking.

Direction involves two forces in tension. On one hand, direction is a result of having *vision*, of seeing where we can go. "Look at that! Let's do it! Let's climb that mountain! Let's swim across the lake! Let's dive into the surf!" On the other hand, there is the importance of *rest,* of identifying with work in progress. Although these may sound diametrically opposed, they are really two complementary forces.

For example, in our body we have muscles working in opposition (in tension) with each other. These muscles give us strength and power in our body, as well as control. We may look at our bicep and focus on that muscle on the top of our arm because that is the one that appears to be the key to our strength. But in order for that muscle to function properly, there is another muscle underneath which is pulling against the bicep. This muscle, as it pulls, creates a tension. That tension, between the top muscle and the bottom muscle, gives us the ability to control just how much strength we use and in what direction we exercise and use that strength. Without this bottom muscle, the bicep is just a big blob. Control and the actual work gets done as we exercise both muscles in tension with one another.

Direction in Leadership

Vision ← → Rest

"Vision" or "rest" leadership style?

When we understand how the two dynamics of vision and rest affect our leadership direction, we will want to exercise them together. Some leaders will find themselves operating closer to "vision" in their style of leadership, others closer to the "rest" dimension. Every leader should understand these dynamics to discover how he leads.

"Vision" often motivates the leader with passion and enthusiasm. *Enthusiasm* means *filled with God, or God in you.* Enthusiasm is not just cheer-leading. Enthusiasm is a genuine filling of God working through us to give us zeal for what we are doing.

Other leaders more motivated to "rest" may not be outwardly excited, but they are still very enthusiastic for what God has called them to do. Their revelation of God is disciplined. The direction that follows comes from being disciplined by an ongoing daily dependency on God to only do the things that He has given them to do.

Leadership groups or ministries that are led only by visionary people tend to really take off with a great sweep of motion, organization and activity. But, they often extend themselves beyond their resources. They commit to too many projects, and there are too many people engaged without adequate support. The group starts collapsing because they do not have the support and the balance they need. The visionary people actually begin unintentionally to dismantle the group.

More than once, I have seen people who were very good church planters, with a high amount of evangelistic anointing in them, build a church up and then attempt to lead it the same way they motivated people to start it. In two years they dismantle it the same way they built it. Why? Because a different anointing of Christ is essential to maintain and build that group. A purely visionary source of direction lacks balance.

A group that only takes the "trust/rest approach" will plod along very, very slowly. They may not be stimulated enough by fresh, inspired vision so they maintain what they are for years. And all the people with drive and determination will go somewhere else because there is no room for them to express vision here. Ideally, what we need is the interaction of both vision and rest so that the group, ministry, or congregation has direction and a sense of rootedness and discipline in hearing God's voice each step of the way.

Vision

Let us look first of all at vision. Vision in leadership is *the capacity of a leader to see ahead to the purposes that God has for himself personally, as a leader, and also for the area of responsibility entrusted to him.* Any time God gives us a vision, it is larger than what we can accomplish by ourselves. It requires the help, gifting, cooperation, support, and prayers of other people in order for it to come to pass.

When I worked at a college, I was associated with a department leader, Bob, who was continually generating new vision and programs to improve our services to teachers. One day he was introducing a new idea to our staff, yet he had no sense of how to translate his idea into action.

As I sat in the meeting, I saw Bob struggling, and I saw a way to pull it all together for him. I volunteered to use the chalkboard to write down some of the ways the staff could see us implementing his ideas. He breathed a sigh of relief and turned the meeting over to me. Thirty minutes later, we had collected and evaluated our ideas. Then we chose a plan of action together.

For several months after that, Bob kept complimenting me for my ability to do what he could not do. I was glad to see him succeed; my skills were complementary to his. It was equally true that I could not do what he did so well.

A leader's vision will always be an imposition on other people. If one is going to accomplish the vision, other people will need to help pay the price. God, in His unique way, gives us something bigger than what we can do by ourselves—therefore preparing us to be knit together with the Body of Christ. The rest of the Body has exactly what we need to make up for what we lack!

Vision is much more than just saying, "Let's have a bigger group." Although it is always God's purpose to expand His kingdom to more people, being larger for the sake of numbers so it can inflate our ego is the wrong direction to take. Such vision is inadequate. If people come into our group, they want us to lead them somewhere and do something that is beneficial for them. We will be blessed if they love, appreciate, cooperate, and honor us, but they are not there for *us*. *We* are there for them. A leader needs to be able to see which vision is from God and not merely reproduce something bigger and better than what someone else is already doing.

Proverbs 29 puts it this way in verse 18, *"Where there is no vision, the people are unrestrained."* More specifically, we could render that passage this way: "Without a redemptive revelation from God, the people wander aimlessly." The heart of vision is not merely an idea of something to achieve—it is seeing and meeting God so He transforms us to do what He wants done. This kind of Biblical vision drives and moves a leader with a passion to see God's will done.

Vision comes from a personal revelation from God

Paul said, *"I pray that the eyes of your heart may be enlightened, so that you may know what is the hope of His calling"* (Ephesians 1:18). Another more literal rendering of that verse would be, "I pray that the vision of your deep thought will be flooded with light." In other words, as we meditate upon what God has for us and who we are in Him, God is shedding light on our hearts for us to see His purposes.

We need to cultivate a time of listening to the Lord. There are times we need to get quiet and let God speak to us. Another good time for the light to shine is when we are meditating on God's Word. As a leader spends time with Him, he will gain a capacity to foresee the purposes of God. His passion will begin to motivate others to do the same. A leader need not herd people like cows, saying, "Come on, you guys, why aren't you getting with it?" A true leader leads by being the most passionate person about his "direction."

We, as leaders, influence the release of giving financially in our fellowship. I like to put it this way: As a leader, I may not be able to be the one who gives the most in amount, but I should always be leading in the spirit of generosity and liberality. I should be a leader in giving to the work of which I am a part. I should have a mind-set of wanting to give to see this vision come to pass. I should be sacrificial in giving in ways that are sacrificial for me. When I do that as a leader, it releases that spirit of generosity to the whole group. It is not only saying to people, "Give so that we can fulfill our vision." It is giving, and letting the impartation of generosity saturate the group.

Apostle Paul, an example of a visionary leader

Apostle Paul was a great visionary leader who had a strong sense of direction. He knew who he was and was bold in the face of opposition because he knew the direction he was taking. A leader does not need to have the same kind of personality Paul had, but he illustrates the principle of a visionary leader.

In Acts 26:15-17, Paul was in Caesarea under the custody of the military, explaining his story to King Agrippa about the vision God gave him for ministry. He boldly relates his experience with God on the road to Damascus,

> *"And I said, 'Who art thou, Lord?' And the Lord said, 'I am Jesus whom you are persecuting. But arise, and stand on your feet; for this purpose I have appeared to you, to appoint you a minister and a witness not only to the things which you have seen, but also to the things in which I will appear to you; delivering you from the Jewish people and from the Gentiles, to whom I am sending you.'"*

That is what you call a mixed message! Jesus said He would deliver Paul from the people to whom he was sending him. If Paul thought about it, he had to realize there must be some kind of trouble up ahead. These people were going to react to his direction. But Jesus was sending Paul to *"open their eyes so that they may turn from darkness to light and from the dominion of Satan to God, in order that they may receive forgiveness of sins and an inheritance among those who have been sanctified by faith in Me [Jesus]"* (v. 18).

What a vision! Paul was driven by this passion in his heart. That is what kept him going from place to place. He had a vision, which came from a revelation in meeting God. When we meet God in the intimacy of worship, listening prayer, and of hearing His voice through His Word, we, too, will receive a vision.

One time as some brothers prayed for me, I felt the Lord speak to me and give me a vision for changing the literature piece that I write by calling it *"Moments with the Father."* It was not a spectacular revelation, but a vision, nevertheless, of something He wanted done. I received this vision while I was in a place of meeting with Him.

Paul was able to testify to King Agrippa,

"I did not prove disobedient to the heavenly vision, but kept declaring both to those of Damascus first, and also at Jerusalem and then throughout all the region of Judea, and even to the Gentiles, that they should repent and turn to God, performing deeds appropriate to repentance" (Acts 26:19-20).

As Paul took a step and called forth that vision, it led him from place to place, culture to culture and nation to nation. So on one hand, direction involves having the vision and passion to do something and to be something. But there is a complementary dimension to vision. It is called rest.

Rest

Rest is *the capacity of a leader to trust and obey God apart from willful striving.* "Willful striving" is pressing our will to make something happen or have it our own way. Conflicts occur in relationships where one person forces his will on another. Rest is the absence of that inner striving to make it come out our way. We can rest because we know who we are and the direction we are taking.

When we are not quite sure who we are or do not feel secure in the vision and direction we are going, we may have to push and make something happen to somehow "save face" for our identity and reputation. When we are at rest, however, we can completely trust God to do what He has said He will do in the vision. Hebrews 4 tells us the children of Israel did not enter into their rest, resulting in not receiving the fulfillment of the vision of getting to the Promised Land. Because of disobedience and unbelief, they failed to enter into God's rest.

There remains, therefore, a sabbath rest for the people of God. Those who have entered God's rest also relax from their work as God did from His. By obeying what God has said and doing only what He has placed in our heart to do, we enter into rest. We trust that God will do His part if we simply obey the part He has given us to do.

If we press our willful desires, it removes the opportunity for people to directly meet God in reference to this vision. When we are at rest, persons in our sphere of influence need to deal with the question: "Well, is this of God, or not?" Sometimes the Holy Spirit begins dealing with them in terms of their readiness to respond to the same vision.

How to experience rest

We come to complete rest when we let our hearts be totally opened up before the Lord. Hebrews 4:12 says,

> *"For the word of God is living and active and sharper than any two-edged sword, and piercing as far as the division of soul and spirit, of both joints and marrow, and able to judge the thoughts and intentions of the heart."*

As we allow His Word to penetrate our innermost being and reveal who He says we are and the direction we are to take, all selfishness, willfulness, contention, conflict and fear of others is cut away.

Jesus ministered this very way. In John 5, we see He did only the works His Father gave Him to do. He spoke only the words the Father gave Him to speak—not in some robotic, mechanical way, but out of an intimate and energized relationship. When Jesus spent those intimate moments in listening prayer, He knew the vision. He knew the Father's heart. He didn't have to strive to help it occur.

We know that not everyone that could have been healed was healed during the years of Jesus' ministry. There were plenty of sick people left over to whom the disciples ministered. Even so, Jesus could tell His Father an amazing thing about His ministry here on earth,

> " . . . *having accomplished the work which Thou hast given Me to do"* (John 17:4).

There were many people still to be led. There were many ministry needs still to be touched. Still, Jesus was able to say with clarity of heart, "I have done everything that You gave Me to do." You see, He knew that everything, given into His hands, had been completed. We may paraphrase what He said like this, "I have imparted to these disciples every word, every instruction, every demonstration, every example that You have given Me to do. Now, they are ready to step out on their own in a different kind of relationship with You through the Holy Spirit."

Jesus accomplished the work He had been given to do before He went on the cross. Because He was bringing His earthly leadership ministry to a close, He could testify in this way. That is called rest. Rest is knowing as we walk through our day, we are doing just what the Father wants us to do. Rest comes out of the intimacy and obedience in our experience with God.

Wait on Him

There is a powerful promise in Isaiah 64:4 that says God "acts in behalf of the one who waits for Him." Waiting, of course, is leaning upon Him, like a vine growing up around a large oak tree. The oak tree supports the vine. The vine is depending upon, and entwined around, the oak tree.

To wait is to entwine ourselves around the Lord and receive our strength from who He is and who we are with Him. To wait is to spend time listening and receiving His strength, vision, and passion. To wait is to be prepared like a waiter or waitress in a restaurant, ready to serve. It's an attitude of, "I am listening, ready to do your bidding."

God promises He will act on behalf of those who wait for Him. Many times when we take the time to wait, we could be doing a lot of other things. We could be checking off that long overdue "to do" list. But, when we take the time to wait on Him, God promises to arrange, make efficient, and take care of the things that we have entrusted to Him. He acts on our behalf.

Summary

A healthy leader has a sense of direction, or purpose. This direction, coming from a personal revelation from God, involves the tension between vision and rest. Our direction might come out of the inspiration and passion of "vision," or our direction may come from the "rest" of hearing God speak to us. As such, we obey what He says with the peace of knowing we are going to fulfill His purpose and lead in the right direction.

Within any leadership team some leaders are more visionary, and others are more oriented to the hearing/obeying approach. A pastor I have related to personally for over a decade struggled with the fact that he is not a visionary leader. He does not normally get inspired with great ideas of how his church can be moving on in God. He is a father who has a good family, loves his flock, loves to give, bless, and visit the "down-and-outers."

People respond positively to him because he is a wonderful father to them. But when he goes to seminars instructing one as to how to lead a church, and there is talk about vision, he feels very inadequate. He knows he is not a boss—he is a foreman. He loves to direct the things he is responsible for, but coming up with new ideas is not his "thing."

He tried desperately to be a leader with vision but just could not cook it up. As we worked with this pastor's team, we discovered that the Lord had blessed him with a team member who was very visionary. We helped the team to see how to rally around their pastor and support him in discerning the vision, but then totally commit to helping the pastor fulfill what God has given him (them) to do.

A healthy leader has a sense of direction, or purpose. This direction, coming from a personal revelation from God, involves the tension between vision and rest. Our direction might come out of the inspiration and passion of "vision," or our direction may come from the "rest" of hearing God speak to us.

This pastor now takes time regularly to listen to God and hear and obey what He tells him to do. He gets a sense of direction for the congregation that way, and the visionary people then take what God has been saying and put the passion and enthusiasm into it. It is working very well. The team respects the pastor as the father who is given the stewardship of that congregation.

So we see that direction can come from the inspiration of seeing the purposes of God, or it can come out of the rest of hearing and obeying what God is saying. Dr. Cho, who leads the largest church in the world, shows us how one can function in both dimensions of this dynamic tension of direction in a leader's life. He keeps getting a bigger and bigger vision as his church grows and grows.

He gave 50,000 members away to a pastor to start a new church, and Dr. Cho's church kept growing and growing. What is the secret? He says, "I pray, and I obey." We see, in him, one who is able to function with direction as a leader in both dimensions of vision and rest.

Chapter Two
Reflections

Take a moment to examine your leadership style in establishing direction.

1. Is my primary source of **direction** as a leader from **vision**—seeing the purposes of God for my area of responsibility?

   [or]

   Is my primary source of **direction** derived from **rest**—hearing and obeying God's desires, trusting Him apart from willful striving?

2. Where do I find myself on the continuum of direction?

   Vision_____Rest

3. In what regard do I need to grow in my level of vision . . . or my capacity to rest?

4. What is the clear written purpose statement of direction for my area of leadership responsibility?

Chapter 3

Identity
In Leadership

Descartes reasoned, "I think, therefore, I am." He found proof for his existence, and identity, by considering what was within.

One evening before the worship service began, I walked purposefully across the front of the meeting room to chat with a friend for a moment. After the service, an unfamiliar man, several years older than myself, approached me. As we shook hands, he asked, "Are you Jonas Yoder's son?" I acknowledged that, in fact, I am.

My new acquaintance went on to explain that my father, a teacher, had provided transportation for him to school. When he saw me striding across the front of the church, he explained, I walked just like my father. My identity was clearly linked to the influence of my father's genetic code and modeling.

Jesus had His identity confirmed from One who identified with Him in love, "This is My Beloved Son in whom I am well pleased" (Matthew 3:17).

The second dynamic of being a healthy individual as a leader is *having a clear sense of identity.* Healthy individuality as a leader is having a clear sense of identity as to who we are and what God has made us to be as leaders. People, who are called and gifted by God in leadership, possess certain differences from the people they lead. In the body of Christ, we maintain the sense that we are distinctive members of the body, and each member has a different function. Being members together in Christ's body does not mean that we are all alike. Leaders need to lead, hence they are different from the people being led with respect to their responsibility and capacity to lead.

One of the tendencies, particularly of young men entering into leadership, is they hesitate to take charge and truly lead. I began my teaching career as a sixth grade teacher, and my philosophy coming out of college was, "I just want to be a friend to these students." But I was not hired by the school board or their parents to be their friend. I was there to provide a structured environment where the students could attain certain objectives and purposes. As you can well imagine, after three weeks of being their friend, I needed to redefine my identity as a teacher and embrace a leadership role in the classroom.

The purpose one has as a teacher is different from that of the students. The difference is the teacher is the one who is responsible to stimulate their learning and to guide them into various applications of truth.

A mistake that cell group leaders in a church can make is to say, "Well, I am just one of the bunch; let us have a nice time of fellowship with these people and just be their friends."

A cell group leader is there to lead the cell group. This certainly does not mean to say that the cell group leader should be unfriendly or to feel better than the people he leads, but he is to be *different.* When a leader denies that he or she is a different person because of that leadership responsibility, confusion is bred in the group one leads. Such a leader is telling the people, "I am not what you think I am. I am not what you think I am supposed to be. I am really not leading, even though that is what you want me to do."

Jesus was clearly different from His disciples. He was called to walk a different road from the disciples. Jesus operated independently of the masses. As He rode triumphantly toward Jerusalem with multitudes praising God joyfully with a loud voice, Jesus wept when He saw Jerusalem. His identity was not found in the support of the masses nor was His value measured by the level of criticism of the Pharisees. As leaders, God puts a difference in us—that very difference is what the group needs from us. For example, husbands should not try to be like their wives. Knowing their differences and when to exercise and manifest those differences helps the couple to interact effectively. A wise, healthy leader is able to maintain a distinct identity, separate from those he leads.

Concept of Detachment

A leader must learn to detach himself or herself from the burdens, emotions, struggles, weights, conflicts, pressures, weariness, and the monotony of leading the group. Detachment is important because a leader needs to be able to back off from his responsibilities and take a fresh look at them.

To detach is that capacity to remain above the circumstances in our perspective. It is to disengage from being entangled by everything that is going on. To detach is to avoid getting caught up in the problems to the extent that we cannot function any more as leaders. Like an eagle that rises above the storm and looks down and gains perspective, to detach is to pull away from the leadership responsibility and get a fresh perspective.

If a leader cannot detach, he will burn out. God himself rested and refreshed Himself at the conclusion of creation, not because He was inadequate, but He was setting in motion a wise and loving principle for His creatures. The sabbath principle, whether applied on a daily, weekly, monthly, annual, or seasonal basis in our work is a very important principle. We need to be able to emotionally detach, so our leadership responsibility does not run us. Instead, we are functioning in obedience to God in our leadership.

What are some ways that we can do this? We can take a vacation, whether it is a five-minute vacation on Wednesday afternoon, or a two-week vacation in August. Taking a sabbatical is a way of detaching from the responsibility and gaining a fresh perspective.

There are other ways to detach. We can read about topics unrelated to our leadership responsibility. We can detach through a hobby. As Jesus did, we need to regularly "come apart and rest awhile." In times of sabbath reflection on our work, like Christ, we gain perspective on what the Father is saying and doing. Then with fresh perspective and passion we return to responsibility.

Concept of Affection

Along with the capacity to know ourselves apart from everyone else (knowing how to detach), we need a capacity to fully identify with other people. We call this dimension of our identity as a leader *affection.* Apostle Paul longed for the Philippian church *"with the affection of Christ Jesus"* (Philippians 1:8). To the Thessalonians, Paul testified,

"Having thus a fond affection for you, we were well-pleased to impart to you not only the gospel of

God but also our own lives, because you had become very dear to us" (I Thessalonians 2:8).

We express affection as leaders when we are vulnerable with people. We relate with compassion in times of need and failure. We open our lives to give others strength in situations of adversity. Such warmth and nurturing love builds trust in God and in our leadership.

A healthy person has learned to differentiate himself from others while still giving himself fully in an intimate, caring, personable way to those in his care.

"To differentiate" is to "distinguish that we are different from other people." I am not you. You are not me. As a leader, we must know who we are as distinguished from other people. People who have achieved this task are aware of themselves, their strengths, weaknesses, gifts, and how they fit into the Body of Christ. They know what they can do and what they cannot, or should not, do.

Many years ago, I was involved in a ministry that learned what we were not able to do. It was very valuable. We were not resigning to the thought that we were unable to accomplish certain things. Instead, we were acknowledging only the things God had called us to and that we could do. It was God's way of fitting us into the Body. When a person knows he is distinct from everyone else, he is able to be truly in touch, compassionately, with other people.

Individuate

We use the term *individuate* to describe *the task of becoming an individual.* It is the process of becoming a separate individual from all that has shaped and formed us. A person progressively develops and becomes an individual right from the mother's womb. (If one does not, one does not survive.) As a child is born and grows older, he progressively becomes more and more separate from the things that shaped and formed him. This is the path to becoming a healthy individual emotionally.

Consider this principle in Jesus' life. Like any newborn, He was totally dependent upon His parents to care for and nurture Him. As He grew through the years of childhood, He "... continued to grow and become strong, increasing in wisdom; and the grace of God was upon Him" (Luke 2:40).

At age twelve, He accompanied His parents to the Feast of the Passover in Jerusalem. By this time, He had become much less attached to His parents, for they traveled for a day after the feast before they discovered that He was not among the caravan of relatives. After three days they found Him in the temple, sitting in the midst of the teachers, listening and asking questions.

When His mother expressed the parents' anxious concern over His absence and separation, Jesus replied, *"Why is it that you were looking for Me? Did you not know that I had to be in My Father's house?"* (Luke 2:49). Jesus was defining His identity more with His Heavenly Father and less with His earthly parents. Jesus did continue in subjection to them, yet at the same time He kept *"increasing in wisdom and stature, and in favor with God and men"* (Luke 2:52).

As Jesus entered into His ministry, great multitudes of people followed Him, yet He chose only twelve disciples with whom to be closely associated. In Mark 3:21, we read that when He returned to His home community, people gathered to such an extent that He and the disciples could not even eat a meal. His kinsmen (relatives) came *"to take custody of Him; for they were saying, 'He has lost His senses.'"* The scribes from Jerusalem accused Him of being controlled by a demon.

Finally, His mother and His brothers arrived. They sent word through the crowd, calling Him to come out. When He received the message from the multitude, He looked upon those around Him and said, *"Behold, My mother and My brothers!"* (Mark 3:34).

In this setting, Jesus showed that He had individuated from His parents and family, particularly His mother. In knowing who He was, as separate from His family and kinsmen, He was able to fully identify in an affectionate way with "whoever does the will of God" (Mark 3:35).

Spiritually it is important for us to individuate. We must discover who we are as an individual apart from that which has shaped and formed us. This is why the Bible says that a man shall leave his father and mother and cleave to his wife. If he does not leave, his wife will know. If he does not leave emotionally, it is very frustrating to her because he has not totally separated himself from that which has shaped and formed him.

Most people, when they find out who they are (separate from what has formed them), often choose again many of those formative influences as their own values. How many of us are really a lot like our parents in many of our choices and values because we have chosen those very things for ourselves? We can be very grateful for many of the things that we have been influenced to see and experience so that we can choose them.

If we are going to become spiritual fathers and mothers in God's kingdom and the church, then we have to individuate from those spiritual streams and roots that have shaped and formed our spiritual walk. We have to leave them and cleave to the revelation that God gives us personally and specifically in order for us to be mature and reproduce this revelation in others.

This does not mean we should reject all the teaching we received in the past. But if we are subject to what others say, we will not have the stamina and the boldness to declare, "I say." That is why Paul entreated the church at Ephesus to pray for him so he would speak boldly and confidently (Ephesians 6:20). Paul was not merely asking for more boldness. He was really asking for prayer to be able to speak out in the face of Jewish people the revelation that he had received—that the Gentiles are accepted, too. He was "leaving" his spiritual heritage, and cleaving to the revelation that Christ had shown him.

As leaders, we need to be able to recognize what our roots are (what our heritage is and what has shaped and formed us), be able to build on it, and move beyond it. Those who cannot do this are less likely to stand firm in the midst of controversy.

Consider Jesus and the rich young ruler in Matthew 19:16-18, 20-22. This young man was a person with character, committed to the law, a person who had fulfilled the heritage in which he was walking. He sincerely wanted to know how to inherit eternal life when he asked,

> " 'Teacher, what good thing shall I do that I may obtain eternal life?' And He said to him, 'Why are you asking Me about what is good? There is only One who is good; but if you wish to enter into life, keep the commandments . . . ' The young man said to Him, 'All these things I have kept; what am I still lacking?' Jesus said to him, 'If you wish to be complete, go and sell your possessions and give to the poor, and you shall have treasure in heaven; and come, follow Me.' But when the young man heard this statement, he went away grieved; for he was one who owned much property."

Notice, Jesus did not run down the road and say, "Ah, wait a minute, on second thought, we do need a treasurer. I realize the treasurer I have with me is not as reliable as he could be. I would like you to be the assistant and perhaps we could promote you later." Jesus was not attached to the young ruler's wealth, youthfulness or dedication. Jesus was detached enough from all those things to say, "Here is what you need to do, young man." That is detachment.

In Mark's account of this encounter, he notes that "Jesus felt a love for him" as Jesus put the test of discipleship before him (10:21). That is affection. But the rich young ruler did not make the step. And then Jesus said that it is hard for a rich man to enter into the kingdom of heaven. He did not say it is impossible. Zacchaeus, the tax collector, made it, but it was not easy.

Jesus helped this man clarify who he was and the direction that he could take. Jesus Himself remained clear on who He was and the direction He was taking. As a leader He could say, "Come, follow Me. I have a vision, I have a direction, I have a purpose. I have heard My Father's voice. I know what I am going to do. I am going to obey Him. I am only speaking and doing the things He has given Me to speak and to do."

In Jesus, we see a healthy leader is able to maintain a distinct identity separate from those he leads. In so doing, he can separate himself from all of the responsibility and get a fresh look at it, and yet give himself or herself fully in a caring, warm way to any individual under his care.

In other words, for a leader to detach is to be like the eagle, soaring above one's area of responsibility to see it from a different perspective. To show affection is to be like a mother hen, being present to closely guard, nurture, and support the persons in our sphere of influence.

Leaders need to know which of these two dimensions of identity they need to embrace more fully—the principle of detachment,

Identity In Leadership / 51

or the principle of affection. The clarity of a leader's identity affects those he leads. When we hesitate to declare ourselves (by hesitating to take that step forward in what we believe God is telling us to do), everyone is waiting for us. In the midst of that pausing and tentativeness, unnecessary conflict erupts because we have not taken clear steps.

Calvin was a pastor who tried to keep the congregation in the denomination while speaking out prophetically about the issues. Gradually, he was positioned in the middle between those in his congregation who wanted to leave the denomination and those who wanted to stay. Of those who wanted to stay, some were concerned about the issues and others were not.

Calvin sought to keep everyone together while at the same time reinforcing the viewpoint of all the different groups in the congregation. The conflict only intensified–and turned on him. As a result, some families began to leave the congregation. Others began the campaign to remove the pastor.

A visiting team was invited to help the congregation review the issues and chart a course of action. One of the team members challenged Calvin to step forward, declare who he was, and the direction he was taking. The double-mindedness had to stop.

When Calvin took a clear stand personally, and compassionately loved all of the people, then individuals were able to define more clearly the path they were to take. While some additional persons left the congregation, the congregation began to stabilize and move forward with its mission.

The more a leader knows who he is, the more he or she can be comfortable with other people being who they are. In turn, they will receive that affirmation and release in becoming whom God has intended them to be.

Jesus is husbanding us as His wife, the Church. He is causing us to grow and move forward in His purposes simply by His love and affection for us. He is detached. He is not caught up in all the problems we are dealing with. He is interceding. He is spending time with the Father, while we work here on earth. And He is coming back with a fresh perspective on how this earth is to be ruled. That is the big picture. Jesus knows who He is, and the more we see who He is, the more clearly we, as a Church, see ourselves as we are in relationship to Him.

Significance

Each person has two foundational needs as a person: *security* and *significance*. While security comes through affection and represents an assurance that one is loved unconditionally, significance is known in the capacity to make a meaningful and lasting impact upon others.

Because Jesus had an intimate relationship with His heavenly Father, His identity was clearly established. He was secure in His Father's love. He was significant because He was doing only that which the Father was saying or doing. When the Father spoke from heaven saying, *"This is My beloved Son, in whom I am well-pleased* (Matthew 3:17)*,* Jesus had confirmation that He was loved (security) and that He was effective (significance).

Leadership, in essence, is influence; that is, making a meaningful and lasting impact upon others. When a leader has a clear sense that what he or she is doing makes a lasting difference in others, that leader experiences significance.

Yet our sense of significance must have a clear reference point. When a leader does not have a reference point for determining his or her significance in an intimate relationship with God through Christ, that leader begins to search for a reference point, a source, a confirming word of significance. Without a clear reference point for significance, the leader will lack decisiveness and give confusing signals to those who would follow.

When one's sense of significance is threatened, confused, or uncertain, a leader may temporarily cease to provide clear and constructive influence upon others. In some instances, the leader may begin to undermine the relationships and vision that are most important to him in his own attempts to maintain past images of significance.

Wilson was a pastor who struggled with his own sense of worth. After working at a Christian camp as a program director for youth, he took a pastoral position. At first, he was buoyed up by the sense of significance that he was now someone important: he was a pastor! When the resistance to ideas began to increase and he was criticized for his shallowness, he became depressed. To regain his importance, he tried to pattern his ministry after well-known personalities throughout the Body of Christ. As each of these models not only failed to satisfy himself, but also failed to minister to his congregation, his search for significance brought him to a point of brokenness.

Through an experience of personal renewal and counsel from a wise mentor, Wilson was able to discern his true source of security in God's love for him. He was able to see the way God was shaping his identity. His own personal encounter with God (as He is) through the Scriptures, established His identity as *a son of God* (Galatians 4:4-7). Wilson grew in wholeness, as so many leaders today need to do, by embracing this truth rather than trying to be like someone he was not. The identity crisis over his leadership steadily resolved through the spiritual fathering of his mentor. He was able to find both rest and significance in doing what the Father was giving him to do.

One's identity as a leader is truly formed through a personal, intimate relationship with God as Father. As we become established in His love and in the work He has for us to do, we know best who we are. Knowing who we are enables us to differentiate who we are from those we lead and from the work we do. As a result, we can regularly detach from our people and tasks. Just as important, we can freely give ourselves, without fear, to show affection to those we lead.

Chapter Three
Reflections

1. What are the ways in which I regularly detach from my leadership responsibilities? What new means of detachment should I embrace?

2. In what ways do I openly demonstrate affection to those who are in my sphere of influence?

3. To what or to whom am I actually looking for my sense of significance?

4. In what ways do I need to individuate more completely from parents, culture, or spiritual heritage?

Chapter 4

Service
In Leadership

We have learned that one of the dimensions of being a healthy individual, as a leader, is we *have a sense of direction*. The tension between being inspired by vision and being disciplined by an obedient trust and rest in Him keeps us moving forward in a productive way.

Another thing we have observed in a healthy individual is *having a clear sense of identity*; that is, he or she is able to detach from responsibility, gain a fresh perspective and return to that responsibility.

When we are able to pull back, we are then free to fully give ourselves. We can disclose who we are and openly, warmly, and affectionately love those people whom God has entrusted to our care.

Service

Lydia serves as principal of a growing school in Nigeria. She leads in her quiet manner with an underlying strength expressed as a smile. She transitioned from her position as a capable teacher into leadership of the school because she was faithful. Her sense of responsibility, her reliability, her commitment to the vision, and her love for the students and fellow teachers can all be summarized in one word—service.

In addition to a clear sense of identity and direction, a healthy individual needs a third dimension of leadership, namely, "service." Jesus said, "I did not come to be served but to serve." What are the dimensions of effective service in God's kingdom?

Responsibility in our leadership role

There are two basic dimensions that, again, are in tension. The first is "responsibility" and the second "availability." Again, let's place ourselves on this continuum—are we more prone to look at our leadership role as a responsibility or approach it with the attitude of making ourselves available?

Responsibility is *the capacity to capably and faithfully make the right responses within our sphere of influence.* A responsible person has a sense of, "I am capable for this work." Of course, we all realize from time to time that we are doing something for which we do not feel we are an expert. But a responsible person has a sense of "I am capable, I am trained, prepared or supported to do this. With the help of God and my brothers and sisters cooperation I can do it." It is a sense of being capable.

Secondly, responsibility involves being faithful. It is saying, "I will continue in this responsibility until I am clearly released. I will fulfill all the things involved in this responsibility and be faithful to it." If someone is responsible, we can count on them to do the job they have assumed. As leaders, we love to have faithful and responsible people, but it starts with us. We need to be capable and faithful. Responsibility is basically making the right response in situations.

We should ask ourselves, "What would be the proper, Godly, truthful response to this job, task, problem or decision?" All of life involves two dimensions: relationships and tasks. We are either relating to people or working at tasks. Some of us in our personality are more naturally task-oriented—we love to work at things and deal with projects. Others of us are more people-oriented—we love to be with people, to talk and interact. Of course, we all have to deal with both relationships and tasks. As a leader we must mature to the point where we can develop our skills in both tasks and relationships. The wise leader will recognize the people God has given to him that complement him as he works at tasks and relationships.

Leadership is influence. When we lead, we are influencing a group to move from point A to point B. The part of our world that God has given us to influence—our community, congregation, cell groups, staff, business—is our sphere of influence. In II Corinthians, chapter 10, Paul is clearly aware of this, as someone who was called to go to the Gentiles and to many nations. He still had a clearly defined sense of his area of responsibility.

We often read this 10th chapter in regard to spiritual warfare. But note, immediately following the discussion of how we deal with thoughts and ideas that are contrary to Christ, Paul begins to discuss his realm of responsibility. One of the keys in spiritual warfare is that we have authority and influence in our sphere of responsibility. Notice what he says in verses 13 through 18,

> *"But we will not boast beyond our measure, but within the measure of the sphere which God apportioned to us as a measure, to reach even as far as you.*

For we are not overextending ourselves, as if we did not reach to you, for we were the first to come even as far as you in the gospel of Christ; not boasting beyond our measure, that is, in other men's labors, but with the hope that as your faith grows, we shall be, within our sphere, enlarged even more by you, so as to preach the gospel even to the regions beyond you, and not to boast in what has been accomplished in the sphere of another. But he who boasts, let him boast in the Lord. For not he who commends himself is approved, but whom the Lord commends."

Metron—an area of influence

The Greek word for *measure* in this passage of Scripture is *metron.* A metron is a sphere, or measure, or area of influence. For example, if you were a farmer, you have a certain amount of land you cultivate. It is under your influence and power to decide what crops will be in those fields this year. That is your metron. You do not have authority or the right to decide what is planted in your neighbor's field. That is his metron.

Your metron, in regard to your life, includes many things. Your metron would include your family and any sense of responsibility you have for those people and their activities. Your metron includes any responsibility you have in a job—your responsibility to take care of a department, run a machine, file a report and so forth. Your metron may also include your ministry responsibility, the department, cell group and every aspect of ministry for which you are responsible.

When we work with others, the metrons sometimes overlap. For example, on a leadership team in a congregation, we share a metron together. But, within that leadership team there may be different metrons. That is, the lead elder or pastor has a different metron from the other members of the leadership team.

A person needs to give the proper responses to his or her area of responsibility. For example, God gives Brother Martie wisdom and insight about how to teach his class. That is his metron. Of course, if Martie would bring his metron to me, and say, "Brother Keith, I am dealing with a problem within my metron. I am submitting my metron to you for counsel about what to do with this matter." Then God would give me grace and vision along with Martie to come up with wisdom for that matter within his metron. But I only speak into his metron because he has presented it to me. It is improper to grasp it and take it away from him.

That is why guerrilla warfare never works within a congregation! It is not within the individual member's metron to decide what is going to happen in the whole congregation. That metron is given to the leaders to cover and watch over. A leader will involve the participation of the people within the metron so that his decision is the most sensitive, affectionate, wise and broad-based as possible. But the metron, vision, and the discernment for the congregation as a whole will primarily be given to whomever is responsible within that congregation.

For example, I was serving on an elders team, and we had delegated a lot of responsibility to other smaller metrons within the congregation. One time when we were meeting as elders in our metron, overseeing the whole congregation, a matter was brought to our level of responsibility by a smaller "Christian education" metron within the congregation. Those leading this metron presented us with a particular problem and asked us if we would tell them what to do about it. We struggled for a half an hour or more trying to make a decision about this small matter. Then we made a decision, telling them what to do. But it was a bad decision. It didn't work. Why? We were not supposed to be making that decision.

That decision belonged to that metron. They needed a little help with it, but the grace to decide the matter was there for them to make, and they should have made it.

Some leaders do not lead decisively in their metron because they do not realize it is theirs. As a leader of a metron, God is going to place most of the vision and direction into that person's heart for that metron. The sooner we know who we are and the direction we are taking, then we can help our group to hear, discern and embrace it together.

Three things giving a leader authority in his metron

What gives us authority and anointing in our metron? Note the triangle in the diagram below. One of the things that gives us authority and releases anointing in our metron is simply the position we have—our appointed role as elder, director, overseer, leader, etc. This is one side of the triangle. The position itself carries an anointing to fulfill the responsibility.

A second side of the triangle is the aspect of our anointing that comes from the gifting we have, whether it be the gift of mercy, the anointing of a pastor or the gift of prophecy, etc. So the position we have gives us authority, and the anointing of our gift makes a place for us.

The third dimension that is most crucial and is the foundation of this triangle is fellowship with God. Intimacy, prayer and communion with God releases the anointing within us that brings stability and support to the fact that we are in the leadership position.

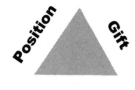

Fellowship

This may explain why a leader seems to have a great anointing on his ministry with wonderful gifts flowing and powerful things happening, then it is revealed that his life is in shambles. If he is a hypocrite, why does God heal dozens of people through this person's ministry?

First of all, this kind of leader is operating only in the anointing of his position and gifts. He has allowed his fellowship with God to diminish and dry out. God still honors the position and gifting, but if he does not have the spiritual foundation, sooner or later his leadership—and his life—will collapse.

So in our metron, if we maintain an intimate fellowship with God, it does not matter if we do not have the gifts that somebody else has. It does not matter that we do not have the position to influence people as broadly as we would like. We need to maintain fellowship with God. The gifts will make a way for us, and God will appoint us according to the responsibility He has intended for us.

The stronger the intimate relationship with God, the more vibrant the message will be coming from our hearts, drawing the people around us to say, "We need to give this person a more responsible position. There is so much life of Christ in him, we need to be giving him more responsibility in Christ."

God will give us vision for our metrons—those areas of our responsibility. Unless we define who we are and the direction we are going to go within that metron, it cannot move ahead—whether it is our business, ministry or family. When we define who we are and the direction we are going within our metron, we make progress with our vision. Remember, we are not trying to be like someone else. We need to define who *we* are. We do not seek humanistic self-esteem, rather we have Christ-esteem, which is Christ shaping and forming us in His image. That is who we are—and who we are becoming.

Availability in our leadership role

The other side of the tension in service is being "available." *Availability* is *the capacity to be attentive*. Those who have the motivation gift of serving are especially alert and attentive to the needs of others. We need to be attentive to those who are over us in responsibility, whose metron covers our metron. We need to ask, "What can we do to serve, honor, bless and support them in their vision?"

At the same time, we need to be attentive, open and available to those people around us who need what God has given us. So whether it is someone over us or under us in authority and responsibility, we need to be attentive in both directions in our lives. Usually there are more people drawing from us in our lives and just a few that give us input. We need to make sure we have those few people that we can look to and draw from, so that our metron can increase and give life to many around us.

Let us again notice the attitude behind availability in Isaiah 6. King Uzziah, a great king, had died. Young Isaiah was seeking God during this time of change in leadership when he received a vision of God on the throne. Radiant, brilliant beings, called seraphims, were shielding their eyes from God's brightness and worshiping Him, saying, "Holy, holy, holy."

All Isaiah the prophet (who apparently was highly skilled and trained in the knowledge of his day), could say was, "Woe is me." He needed a touch of God's fire and holiness. He saw his total inability and uncleanness in light of God's holiness. When one of the seraphims touched his lips, Isaiah could only then get in touch with the heart, vision, purpose and direction of God. He could over-hear God's heart saying, "Who will go? Whom can we send? Who is available?" His transformed heart could then readily respond as it did, "Here am I, send me."

A heart that has been transformed by the presence of God has the grace within to say, "I will do it." We can then be available with a sense that God has so transformed and overwhelmed us, that something has to be released. All this grace in us has to go somewhere, so we can say, "Whatever it is Lord, I will do it." It does not matter what it is, because we are serving a Holy God.

Gauging our availability and responsibility

In this divine dimension of service we need to be responsible people. Here are some questions we need to ask ourselves:

Can people count on us to be capable? Are we capable for the responsibility we have? Do we pursue personal growth in the skills we know are required of us and our metron?

Are we responsive to the problems that come up, or do we just sweep them under the rug? Do we try to solve problems by avoiding them and hoping they will go away? That is not being responsible in our metrons. Are we faithful? Are we sticking to what we started until it is completed?

Are we making the necessary responses to the people in our metron with whom relationships are to be cultivated? Are we trying to cultivate relationships on an intimate level with too many people in our metron, therefore not doing sufficient relationship-building with the few people to whom we are especially called?

Jesus related to twelve disciples. When we explore the universe with a microscope to the smallest particles in a configuration, the largest number of elements that are meaningfully related into a compound is twelve. No matter how far we reach into the universe with our telescopes and our radio telescopes, the largest number of meaningfully related galaxies and elements is twelve.

I found in my own life that twelve is about the maximum capacity of relationships that I can be meaningfully involved with at any one time. If someone is getting closer to me, then someone else is getting farther away from me. When that is happening, I need to talk about the transitions with the people involved. It is important to process the relationship and not just let things fall apart. When a new baby enters a family, children should be told how the new baby may change the amount of time family members spend together, for example.

When we are healthy as individuals, we will be aware of God's affirmation of what He has asked us to do. We will be aware of God's holiness. We will gauge our availability and our responsibility according to what He has spoken to us. When we go through a transition as leaders, it can be difficult emotionally because our identity has been connected to what we have been doing. But a healthy individual, in transitions, feels free to go or stay.

In the transitions I have gone through, God has taken me through this process; first, I had to be willing to let go, leave, change responsibility, or lay something down that I had been doing. When I got to the point where I could go, then sometimes I needed to consider the question, "Would I be willing to remain in this responsibility for another year?" When I come to the point in my heart where I am free to go (I do not need to hang on to the security), or I am free to stay (I do not have to do anything different), then I am ready to make the transition, emotionally.

Such a posture shows true maturity. Maturity can be defined in many ways, but in our context *maturity* is *the ability to take responsibility for one's actions and one's own emotional growth.* A child by definition is someone who is dependent upon others. Adults by definition are people who take care of themselves and others. Maturity is reflected in our capacity as leaders to take care of ourselves and take care of the things within our metron. It does not mean that we are not connected to and drawing counsel and life from others, but *emotionally* we are not depending on the group to tell us what to do as the leader. Emotionally, we are not holding back from taking our responsibility in our metron out of fear of what might happen if we take a certain direction.

Humility in a sense is an awareness of our strengths. A humble person knows what one's gifts are and what they are not. We are aware of our strengths, and whatever we get to do is a privilege. We need to embrace the attitude that God has given us the privilege of serving our metron. On the other hand, we are aware of our weaknesses. We are aware of the unclean lips of our people and of ourselves. We need to remain broken in attitude so that we would not assert ourselves beyond the level of God's actual grace working in us.

So again, a healthy leader has a clear sense of responsibility and serves faithfully. He is accessible to those persons within the sphere of influence that God has designated. On the other hand, such a leader restricts his service and accessibility from matters that are not within his metron.

Jesus is our example. He testified, "Father, I have accomplished all of the work which You gave me to do." What a testimony! Paul also concluded his ministry by saying in II Timothy 4:7 (my paraphrase), "I have run the course, I have finished the race, I did it. I have completed all the things that God has put in my charge. And Timothy, I challenge you to do the same."

I realize in my own life and ministry that there are some things that God gave me vision for that I did not do. The opportunity passed, and I will never get to do it again. So I cannot come to the end of my life and say I have accomplished all the work that God gave me to do, but my heart's desire is that as much as possible, from this point on, that will be my true testimony.

So again, a healthy leader has a clear sense of responsibility and serves faithfully. He is accessible to those persons within the sphere of influence that God has designated. On the other hand, such a leader restricts his service and accessibility from matters that are not within his metron.

One discipline exercised by a leader is not to be involved in everything that comes his way. If we are called to be leaders in the kingdom of God, we must take seriously the discipline of not being overinvolved in other activities outside our metron. Whatever God has given us to do in the kingdom, for kingdom purposes, must be a leader's priority.

Concerning priorities, we often say our priorities should be God first, family second and so on. Obviously, there is truth in this statement, but I affirm that *God* is our *only* priority. Within our "God priority" we have a family, a ministry or other metrons. Our family needs to be a part of fulfilling our priority in God. Our church responsibility and whatever vocational metron we have has to be a part of fulfilling our destiny in God. Otherwise, why are we doing it? This removes some of the tension between the church and the family, because both metrons need to be expressions of how we serve God together.

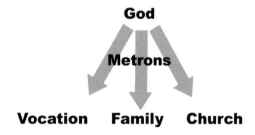

Chapter Four
Reflections

1. For what am I responsible? What is my **metron**?

2. With regard to my responsibilities . . .

   . . . in what ways do I need to develop my **capability**?

   . . . in what ways do I need to become more **faithful**?

3. In what ways do I need to become more **attentive** to the needs and desires . . .

   . . . . of those **to** whom I am responsible?

   . . . . of those **for** whom I am responsible?

Chapter 5

Character
in Leadership

It was the annual assembly of the denomination, and the debate on the floor was focused on the policy regarding communion. Traditionally, the denomination had served communion from a common cup. Under consideration was the recommendation to offer communion in individual cups.

One elderly gentleman spoke passionately for retaining the tradition of the common cup. He gave an eloquent presentation of the symbolism and meaning associated with this practice. The debate concluded and a vote was taken. The moderator announced the results of the vote, indicating that the delegates had approved the change to individual cups.

At that moment, the elderly gentleman, who had so wholeheartedly supported the common cup, asked to speak. He strode to the podium and acknowledged the decision of the assembly, saying, "The next time you serve communion, give me one of those little cups." In a few words, he drew the delegates to unity with the example of his gracious spirit.

The fourth dimension of having a healthy sense of individuality as a leader is character. From an inward and an outward perspective, there are two essential ingredients of character—integrity and our example.

Integrity

Integrity is *the capacity we have as a person to be genuine and real.* It is the capacity to be the same all the way through. What one sees on the outside is what one discovers on the inside. What one sees in private is the same as what one sees in public. A person of integrity is genuine and transparent.

Such a leader is responsible and reliable in words and actions. We say he is "a man of his word" to describe this characteristic. Ecclesiastes 5:4 says we should fulfill the vow we have made. If we have made a vow and it is no longer possible for us to fulfill it, we can still be responsible for having made the vow if we ask for a release from it.

When we ask for release or for forgiveness for not fulfilling a responsibility, we are taking responsibility for it. For example, if I am late to a meeting and I do not say anything to the others by apologizing for being late, I lack integrity. But, if I come to the meeting late and honor the others by saying, "I'm late, will you forgive me for being late?" then I have maintained a level of integrity with regard to the value of being timely.

A leader must be reliable in words and actions. Integrity is very important. We have seen God do a thorough house cleaning on the integrity issue in leadership in His church in recent years. It started with a few prominent television personalities in large ministries. Their obvious lack of integrity had its roots in a lack of fellowship and intimacy with God. When a person ceases to be open before God, he begins living with the deception that he can function on his own with his gifts, power and position.

Why were Adam and Eve hiding in the Garden of Eden? They were hiding from the presence of the Lord, because the presence of the Lord reminded them of their responsibility and sin. We could say that "prayerlessness" is a form of hiding from God. When we do not spend time with Him, we will not feel comfortable in His presence. When we neglect the fellowship aspect of our intimacy with God, we will have problems with integrity issues.

It seems as if the public exposure of certain leaders in the church was just the tip of the iceberg. God went through the church with a cleansing wind and power to purify the reasons ministers are ministers and why leaders are leaders. God's intention is to bring the whole church to integrity so that all members come to a level of integrity in their hearts, not just in outward actions. Integrity of heart continues to be an issue in the church at large.

As leaders, we are not to be as actors on a stage. We lead from the heart, not merely playing a role that is not true to our heart. We *are* compassionate, not acting compassionately. We pray with conviction, not just with a "holy" voice. We speak that which we know experientially, not declaring things to be true that we have not proven ourselves. We are the same *all the way through.*

Integrity of character is what enables us to take a stand on an issue and pursue a certain direction. Integrity is what enables us to take a stand to correct something that needs to be corrected. Because we know there is no chink in our armor, nothing can sneak up behind us. There is no skeleton in our closet. We can stand up and say, "Folks, this is the direction we are going. This is what we believe about this issue," because we have integrity in our own heart.

Our example

The second dimension of character is our example. Our *example* is the *capacity we have to influence other people to cause them to grow and become more like Christ by the very compelling nature of our action and words.* People want to be like someone in whom they see Jesus. When we see a level of holiness in another, we are drawn to be like that person. Example is very powerful, especially when it is joined with the spoken, declared will of God.

Paul tells us that Jesus needs to be our primary example in Philippians 2:5-8,

> *"Have this attitude in yourselves which was also in Christ Jesus, who, although He existed in the form of God, did not regard equality with God a thing to be grasped, but emptied Himself, taking the form of a bondservant, and being made in the likeness of men. And being found in appearance as a man, He humbled Himself by becoming obedient to the point of death, even death on a cross."*

Then Paul gives us another case study of an example of Christlike, self-giving love in verses 25-30,

> *"But I thought it necessary to send you Epaphroditus, my brother and fellow worker and fellow soldier, who is also your messenger and minister to my need; because he was longing for you all and was distressed because you had heard that he was sick. For indeed he was sick to the point of death, but God had mercy on him, and not on him only but also on me, lest I should have sorrow upon sorrow. Therefore I have sent him all the more eagerly in order that when you see him again you may rejoice and I may be less concerned about you. Therefore receive him in the Lord*

with all joy, and hold men like him in high regard; because he came close to death for the work of Christ, risking his life to complete what was deficient in your service to me."

Epaphroditus had the true spirit of the deacon ministry with his serving heart of submission. He saw a need and took initiative to go and help even at a cost and risk of his own life. He saw what was not being fulfilled in the ministry of Paul and stepped in and did it.

When someone says, "Will you help me?" and we respond and do so cheerfully, it is a beautiful picture of Christ's character. But submission, in its fullest and most beautiful expression, occurs without being asked. It is to see a need and offer to help. We need to hold men and women like this in high regard in our fellowship. We need to recognize people who have this spirit in their ministry. Although it is fine to compliment the musician for how beautiful her voice or dress is, we need to recognize those servants that, without being asked, bake pies and drive 50 miles to deliver them.

As a leader, what we affirm in the midst of the assembly tells the people what we believe is really important. Let us be looking for evidence of character we can affirm, rather than performance. If Sister Mary sings with a beautiful voice and ministers Jesus to us, let us affirm her for ministering Jesus to us, not only for how beautiful her voice was. Note the difference. We want to affirm the evidence of Christ at work in our brothers and sisters. We want to uphold character before the people in this way. To do so engages the power of example.

Understanding others

If a leader does not take a stand, he will not go forward; rather, he will give his leadership away to all kinds of ideas, influences or distractions. The sense of group identity will become unclear, and the ministry or business will begin to fall apart.

When we take a stand, we also need to have the capacity to understand others. What does it mean to understand? *Understand* is a combination of two words, the word *under* and the word *stand*. Stand implies the position. "What is your stand on the issue? What do you believe?"

To understand is to get "under" someone else's position to see like they see. If I held up a box that is yellow on one side and brown on the other and asked two people what color it is, I will get two answers. Regina may say it is brown, and Dan, sitting on the opposite side, may say it is yellow. Now we have a difference of understanding about the same thing. From Dan's perspective (the way he sees it), the box is yellow. From Regina's perspective (the way she sees it), the box is brown. Now, who is right? From the way they see it, both are right. It is their perspective, their viewpoint, that makes the difference.

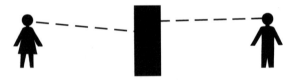

Regina's point of view   Dan's point of view

When we say both are correct perspectives as they see it based on their perception, it does not mean that truth is relative. We should not lean on our own understanding but in all of our ways acknowledge God who knows everything about everything. God gives a way of viewing situations taking into account all perspectives and how they contribute to a full understanding.

Now, if Dan is going to understand Regina's viewpoint on this matter, what must he do? He needs to look at the box by moving to the place from which Regina views it. When he adds Regina's perspective to his own, he discovers it does indeed have two colors. Dan's new perspective comes from seeing another's point of view as well as his own.

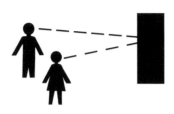

Understanding

That is what it means to understand. To understand is to see it or to hear it the way others hear it. It does not necessarily mean one has to agree totally. If we are going to adopt a common goal, we have to understand each other's point of view and embrace the goal together.

What if Dan has the gift of prophecy and Regina has a gift of mercy? Looking at the same situation, which one is right? What if one person has an apostolic anointing and another person has pastoral anointing? What if one person comes from the east and another from the west? What if one is a man and the other is a woman? In other words, if we are going to hear God together and know His purposes together, as leaders we must have the capacity to identify with the other person and see it the way he sees it.

A leader must be an example in promoting understanding. I may have to move in order to see it the way another person sees it. I may need to humble myself and look at it in exactly the same way they do. I may need to learn to feel what it feels like to "walk in their shoes." Being mature in character gives one the courage to look at a situation the way someone else does and not be threatened in one's own identity.

Responding to reactions

Character is important as leaders respond to the way people react to their direction. When a leader defines who he or she is, and the direction that he or she is taking, then those who are a part of the group may react in some form of resistance. The tendency of the group will be to resist change, even subconsciously, drawing things back to the way they were before the leader declared his identity and direction.

It was one of those letters. Jose could not believe what he was reading, and it was about him! After several paragraphs of slander and the faulty logic of guilt by association, he laid the pages of bitter accusations aside. Inside, he knew the decision he had announced was the best for all parties. Yet to defend himself would only draw the congregation into two sides (Jose was too harsh; Jose was too merciful). Quietly he took strength in that God had called him to be a gentle prophet.

Persons in the group may react by criticizing the leader for who he is. Criticism is a form of "pursuit" of the leader to try to change him to an image more acceptable for those who resist *who the leader is.* Or, some of the group may complain. Complaining is a form of "dependency," presuming that the complainer can keep the leader from imposing change upon the group. Complainers are resisting the *direction the leader is taking.*

When the perceived or "real" leader (some in *positions* of leadership are not the perceived or real leader of the group) defines who he is and the direction he is going, people will generally react. When the leader has integrity, he can take a stand and remain positive in his convictions. He can also seek to bring understanding among those who are seeing the direction from differing perspectives.

In times when people react with criticism or complaining, it is crucial that the leader does not respond in the same way. Rather, the wise leader maintains a sense of poise toward God—open, listening, responsive above all to the One who has given the leader the direction to take.

While the leader stays poised before God, it is important to remain calm, without anxiety before the people. The leader who maintains self-control maintains leadership. Solomon's proverb states it this way, *"He who is slow to anger is better than the mighty, and he who rules his spirit, than he who captures a city* (Proverbs 16:32). The poised leader is not dependent upon pleasing others, nor does he need to manipulate others in order to get them to embrace the direction he is going.

Our presence

A leader with a healthy identity builds *presence* over time through consistent demonstration of integrity in words and actions. In a variety of settings, the leader establishes a sense of presence which is the sum total of all the impressions the leader has made upon others who know him. Presence consists of values, beliefs, choices, decisions, relationships, and respect that are associated with the person. Mistakes (and how they are handled) are remembered as well as achievements. One's position of leadership also contributes to a sense of presence.

Presence may be illustrated from our experience in school. The teacher has a sense of presence in the classroom which consists of respect for the position of teacher, as well as the rules and values the teacher has defined and consistently followed. When the teacher leaves the room temporarily, the students may begin to misbehave. But when a fellow student warns that the teacher is returning, the class returns to normal order just before the teacher enters the room. Without saying a word or doing a thing, the teacher's presence has established definition and direction for the class.

Similarly, when a leader defines who he is and the direction he is going, and people react, it is important to maintain a calm presence without anxiety. This enables the leader to engage the involvement and response of others. Gradually, the people will realize that criticism and complaining cannot control this leader. As people have time to adjust to the stand the leader has taken (on the direction received from the Lord), they will begin to adapt to it and in some measure adopt it. True change is underway. Again, it is critical that the leader not react in the way others are reacting. Instead, he maintains a non-anxious presence and poise toward God.

Change

On the other hand, unless the perceived (or real) leader defines who he is and the direction he is going, the group will not essentially change. The attempts by persons other than the perceived leaders of the group to initiate changes for the whole group will be short-lived at best until things gradually return to "normal."

> A healthy leader has the character that enables him to stand for a cause while at the same time he commands respect as a person. By his poise before God, the clarity of his identity, the definition of his direction, and his presence with the people, he leads the people in the purpose God has for them.

For example, a concerned child has little lasting effect in making changes in his family if the parents do not embrace those changes personally. Lower-level management cannot permanently change a company unless upper-level leadership takes suggestions from management and applies them authoritatively. The mother of the sons of Zebedee could not get her sons positions on either side of Jesus in His kingdom if His Father and He did not agree (Matthew 20:23). Members of a congregation cannot bring about permanent or constructive change in the congregation if that change is not embraced by the real (perceived) leaders.

All of this only reinforces the importance that change is best realized by healthy individuals in positions of leadership who have real and perceived influence. When such leaders define who they are and the direction they are going, then the group can move forward in its vision in constructive ways.

A healthy leader has the character that enables him to stand for a cause while at the same time he commands respect as a person. By his poise before God, the clarity of his identity, the definition of his direction, and his presence with the people, he leads the people in the purpose God has for them. Integrity validates our identity. Example authenticates our direction. Such is the power of character!

Chapter 5
Reflections

1. What adjustments do I need to make to be full of integrity—
   the same all the way through?

2. How shall my words and actions become more compelling as
   an example?

3. Name three specific calming responses to give those who
   react to our sense of direction.

Empowering A New Generation of Leaders

"Will you mentor me?" Each succeeding time I have heard this request, I am more deeply impressed with the weight of it and the potential within it. There is a new generation of men and women, youth, and children looking for persons who can help them become the leaders they are destined to be.

The underlying conviction throughout this book is that effective leaders are persons who have a clear sense of identity and direction. They are persons with a healthy sense of individuality by which they can influence others in a wholesome way.

Emerging leaders are best helped to become effective not by adopting a certain model of leadership nor by embracing a special style of leadership. Rather, they are empowered more fully as their identity is established in personal relationship and revelation from God. Such growth is possible because this is the nature of God's own leadership.

Introduction to God

The bush was burning, but it was not consumed. This attracted Moses' attention. As God spoke to him and called him to lead His people, Moses lacked the confidence and the poise to go. The training in all of the wisdom of Egypt (including models of leadership) was not sufficient. His former efforts to assert himself as a deliverer had failed. His experience in leading his flock of sheep did not give Moses clarity. His identity and capacity to set a direction were inadequate (Exodus 3:13-15).

So God spoke again, "I Am Who I Am." In this statement we see that God is clear as to His identity, and He is sufficient in Himself. He spoke again, *"I Am* has sent . . . you." In these words is the power to set others in motion with a definite direction. To state the obvious, God knows who He is and where He is going.

Emerging leaders are best helped to become effective not by adopting a certain model of leadership nor by embracing a special style of leadership. Rather, they are empowered more fully as their identity is established in personal relationship and revelation from God.

Because of such clear identity and direction, God is able to fully express Himself and identify with others (mankind) in a healthy way. That is, His identity remains clear even as theirs may remain unclear.

"And God, furthermore, said to Moses, "Thus you shall say to the sons of Israel, 'The Lord, the God of your fathers, the God of Abraham, the God of Isaac, and the God of Jacob, has sent me to you.' This is My name forever, and this is My memorial-name to all generations" (Exodus 3:15).

God has chosen to lead His people from generation to generation by identifying with them, with those who trust Him. He reveals Himself to each generation to reproduce faith in them as He did with their forefathers.

Three tools

To empower emerging leaders, we have three tools displayed for us in Hebrews 13:7,

> *"Remember those who led you, who spoke the word of God to you; and considering the result of their conduct, imitate their faith."*

As leaders training emerging leaders, we have a true word of God to explain and proclaim. We do so to bring revelation of God to them.

Second, we have our own example of living according to the revelation we have and give to others.

Third, we model our own trust (rest) in Him and the revelation of His Word. When the result of our faith is Godly, others are urged to imitate our faith. That is, they are also to find their identity in trusting Him and their direction in acting according to His Word.

Godly leadership

Apostle Paul's relationship with the church in Thessalonica models the principles of healthy leadership. To illustrate, look at how they are portrayed in I Thessalonians 2:1-12,

> *"For you yourselves know, brethren, that our coming to you was not in vain, but after we had already suffered and been mistreated in Phillipi, as you know, we had the boldness in our God to speak to you the gospel of God amid much opposition. For our exhortation does not come from error or impurity or by way of deceit; but just as we have been approved by God to be entrusted with the gospel, so we speak, not as pleasing men but God, who examines our hearts. For we never came with flattering speech, as you know, nor with a pretext for greed—God is witness—nor did we*

seek glory from men, either from you or from others, even though as apostles of Christ we might have asserted our authority. But we proved to be gentle among you, as a nursing mother tenderly cares for her own children. Having thus a fond affection for you, we were well-pleased to impart to you not only the gospel of God but also our own lives, because you had become very dear to us. For you recall, brethren, our labor and hardship, how working night and day so as to not be a burden to any of you, we proclaimed to you the gospel of God. You are witnesses, and so is God, how devoutly and uprightly and blamelessly we behaved toward you believers; just as you know how we were exhorting and encouraging and imploring each one of you as a father would his own children, so that you may walk in a manner worthy of the God who calls you into His own kingdom and glory."

What DIRECTION!
Vision!
Paul proclaimed the gospel so that these believers would experience the kingdom and glory of God.
Rest!
No assertion of authority, but gentle nurture.

What IDENTITY!
Detachment!
The Apostle reflects upon his labor and sees it being like a nurturing mother and an exhorting father.
Affection
His relationship was characterized by tender care and fond affection, an open heart, a giving of oneself.

What SERVICE!
Responsibility!
Paul was entrusted with the gospel by God, but chose to not be a burden to any of them.
Availability!
He imparted his own life as well as the gospel message. He served to please God, not men, but he was attentive to their needs like a parent.

What CHARACTER!
Integrity!
There was no error or impurity or deceit in his exhortation. He took a stand amid much opposition. His integrity gave him full authority in their lives.
Example!
He called them to witness his devotion and blameless behavior among them.

The threshold

We are poised at the threshold of a new generation of leaders. Let us not attempt to be conformed outwardly to models and patterns of leadership. Rather, let us draw near to the Father who shapes our identity in a relationship like He has with His Son, Jesus Christ. Let us embrace direction that is generated by a revelation of God's heart and voice for our sphere of responsibility and influence.

Dare to meet God, be an example of faith in Him, and impart your life to others.

"'And their leader shall be one of them, and their ruler shall come forth from their midst; and I will bring him near, and he shall approach Me; for who would dare to risk his life to approach Me?' declares the Lord" (Jeremiah 30:21).

About the author

Keith Yoder is Founder and Executive Director of *Teaching the Word Ministries,* a consultative service to leaders in Christian ministries, congregations and the marketplace. Through prayer, teaching, counsel, writing and mentoring, TTWM presents those whom they serve with the wisdom of God's Word and the Father's heart.

Those who wish to contact the author may call or write Keith at *Teaching the Word Ministries.*

Keith E. Yoder
Teaching the Word Ministries
One Mayfield Drive
Leola, PA 17540

Tele: 717-656-4056
Fax: 717-656-4712
Email: ttwmin@hydrosoft.net
Web: www.ttwm.org